Overcoming Darkness

A Special Collection of Inspirational Readings

John Stuckey, Jr.

Copyright © 2018 by John Stuckey, Jr.

VMH Vikki M. Hankins™Publishing
www.vmhpublishing.com

Without limiting the rights under copyright reserved above, no part of this publication may be reproduced, stored in or introduced into a retrieval system, or transmitted, in any form or by any means.

Manufactured in the United States of America

Hardback ISBN: 978-1-947928-28-2
Paperback ISBN: 978-1-947928-29-9

10 9 8 7 6 5 4 3 2 1

Book Cover Design: Vikki Jones
Book Cover Image: Shutterstock
Interior Images: Unsplash & iStock
Interior Layout Concept: Vikki Jones
Interior Editing: John Stuckey and Kemmeka Davis Stuckey

Publisher's Note:

The publisher is not responsible for the content of this book nor websites, or social media pages (or their content) that are not owned by the publisher.

Forward

My Journey through life has carried me through many challenging situations. Over the past forty years I have been able to chronicle my experiences with these Inspirational Readings. Overcoming Darkness shares my journey in life to finally see my vision and purpose in life.

Overcoming darkness is a daily challenge. We are continually receiving information that our minds must process. TV, Emails, Text Messages, Phone Calls, Social Media, Gaming, are on a list too numerous to mention. What's the right thing to do? Where can I find relief? What should I believe? Where is the Truth? Our Eyes of Understanding are constantly being lulled to sleep. There is a Spiritual War going on.

As we Travel Life's Highway God lets us know our true identity. He shows us that we are more than Conquerors. We have no fear of Evil. No Weapons formed against us shall prosper. We have the courage of the Prophets and great Leaders of the past. God uses strong men and women of faith to carry forth his Plan. Our words have always had the Power to defeat the Enemy. Our words fortify us from the attacks of the Enemy. We are his anointed people, His Kings and Queens.

When we hear Truth it shines light on Darkness. It brings a Peace that surpasses all understanding. Overcoming Darkness will inspire you to stay focused. It will guide you on your quest to seek the Kingdom of God. Overcoming Darkness will be a lamp unto your feet.

These Readings will inspire you to see the God in you. They will give you the vision to become a success at whatever you endeavor. They will inspire you to reach into your mind and see the light that shines within you.

We encourage you to use Overcoming Darkness for Study, Praise and Inspiration. Search the Scriptures on any of the Topics to seek the Truth. The Truth will set you Free.

Overcoming Darkness

READINGS

1. We've Been in the Darkness too Long
2. Life
3. The Fears
4. Never Weaken
5. What is This
6. Get Close to God
7. Walking the Line
8. What God Do You Serve
9. Believe What You See
10. Birds of a Feather
11. Come Together
12. Priceless Gift
13. The Road Less Travelled
14. Mr. Law
15. Love Conquers All
16. Peace
17. A Thinker
18. Push On
19. Up Jumps the Devil
20. All We Need
21. The Art of Giving
22. Love
23. Checked Out of Confusion

READINGS CONT.

24. Clean Up
25. Anger
26. Everything Has Balance
27. A Better Way
28. Let Them Talk
29. Evil
30. Temptation
31. Mighty Dollar
32. Just For Me
33. The Teacher
34. Thoughts
35. Greatest Gift
36. Face of God
37. Happiness
38. Year of Jubilee
39. A Writer's Song
40. A King
41. A Queen

WE'VE BEEN IN THE DARKNESS TOO LONG

Cutting corners
Selling souls
This has taken a mighty toll
We've been in the darkness too long

Fighting for pennies
Conning for control
Is this how to reach a goal
We've been in the darkness too long

Back stabbing
Lying and deceit
One day for sure
Our Creator we must meet
We've been in the darkness too long

Generation after generation
The enemy's cure prevails
Having us believe in nothing but fairy tales
We've been in the darkness too long

We've got to see the light
And let His spirit in our Life
We've been in the darkness too long

LIFE

If there was no sun
How could we exist
If there was not life
What would we miss

If there was no water
What would we drink
If we had no mind
How could we think

If there was no rain
How could a flower grow
If we had no thoughts
What would we know

If there was no moon
Would there be an earth
If there were no mothers
Who would give birth

All the blessings in life
God gives to us each day
Showing all mankind that
His word is the way

THE FEARS

The fear of man
Is the pitfall of life
For the fear of man
Can only bring you strife

The fear of poverty
Is the pain of poverty
But strong belief
Will give you relief

The fear of failure
Is failure at hand
But to conquer failure
Is the right to be a man

The fear of bad health
Is the sickness you receive
So the fear of bad health
You can not believe

The fear of death
Is the anxiety of life
For death may come
But keep it out of sight

The fears and hatred
Control the mind
From the feeling of knowing
God's glory divine

NEVER WEAKEN

Never weaken
Never sway
Just believe in His promises
Trust in His word every day

Reach for the sky
No force can deny
His Grace is sufficient
For just you and I

The road may seem tough
Sometimes it gets rough
No cross, no crown
For me, that's good enough

Never weaken
Never sway
For His mercy and kindness
Will brighten any day

WHAT IS THIS

Things coming down
You getting the runaround
There is no answer to be found
It's the enemy that you feel

Smiling faces telling lies
Sounds good my friend
Now your money is real tight
You know that ain't right
It's the enemy that you feel

Need some more work
Everybody is going berserk
Ambiguous words not real
It's the enemy that you feel

It's the enemy my friend
When business you gotta tend
It's the enemy my friend
When His rules you gotta mend

Watch Listen and Pray
You will Beat the Enemy Today
What is this but God's refinement
Touching us in a very loving way

GET CLOSE TO GOD

Get close to God
And He'll get close to you
He'll help fight your battles
And give wisdom in all that you do

Get close to God
And draw from his mind
For it is only He
Who holds the secrets of time

Get close to God
In secret prayer
Ask Him how, when and where
And He'll get you there

Get close to God
To use all his might
Follow our message
To keep God in sight

Get close to God
He is in every town
For it is only He
That makes the world go around

Get close to God
It will give us lasting grace
Turn away
You will loose the race

WALKING THE LINE

The path of right and wrong
Is ever present and near
It's only for those
Who have an ear to hear

When life tries to take away
Your very existence
Our human instincts
Are to fight with all resistance

Some will cross the line
And lose their way
Thank God for his judgment
To keep us on his narrow way

It's a thin line
Between Love and Hate
So, of its fruits
We cannot partake

Only the strong survive
With strength and might
Love, Patience, and Kindness
Are our weapons in the fight

WHAT GOD DO YOU SERVE

What God do you serve?
Is it the god that promotes sins
Is it the God of false idols
Or belief in other men

What God do you serve?
Is it the god of envy and greed
Or is it the God that supplies
Your every want and need

What God do you serve?
Is it the god of cars and fine dress
Or is it the God that keeps you
Working at your best

What God do you serve?
Is it the god of alcohol and smoke
or is it the God that fulfills
Everyone of your hopes

What God do you serve?
It is the god of money and pleasures
Or it is the God
Who owns all of life's treasures

BELIEVE WHAT YOU SEE

Sometimes in life
It is hard to see
The fortunes of life
Traveling to your destiny

Some may call it luck
Some may call it fame
It is still your destiny
By any other name

Believe what you see
Always be on bended knee
For the fortunes of life
He controls your destiny

Rise above the others
Work in harmony
When you let God in
He will be your best friend

Believe what you see
Always reach your destiny
His Blessings are with you
For all the world to see

BIRDS OF A FEATHER

Birds of a Feather
They flock together
Through any Storm
And any type of weather

They spread their wings
To form Victory
Oh what a sight
For our eyes to see

Birds of a Feather
Always keep their formation
A God given gift
Since the beginning of Creation

They travel far and near
Never concerned about fear
They always hear the Truth
Ringing in their ear

Birds of a Feather
Hear the same song
They follow the message
And stay away from all harm

COME TOGETHER

Come together
All the people in every land
Come together all people
In harmony let us stand

For united we stand
Divided we fall
We all must come together
We all must stand tall

All the people
Gotta take a stand
Spreading our message
Across the land

Red, yellow, green or blue
What does one's color
Mean to you

Color always just gets in the way
Of all mankind brothers
Experiencing some love today

PRICELESS GIFT

You can steal an idea
But you can't steal a thought
And without wisdom and knowledge
The idea is for naught

Ideas and thoughts
Are always being bought
But wisdom and knowledge
Are what should be sought

Ideas and thoughts
Are a personal part of you
You show them
In all you say and do

Man has tried
To steal ideas before
That's like telling Mother Nature
To grow an apple without a core

Wisdom and knowledge
Bring ideas and thoughts
Without wisdom and knowledge
An idea is for naught

THE ROAD LESS TRAVELLED

The road less traveled
Far and near
Singing voices of love
Ringing in my ear

Being always mindful of his cheer
Being prayerful for his promises always near
Being overwhelmed by his shining glory
Being blessed to tell the story

The road less traveled
Not a crowded highway
Knowing tomorrow becomes yesterday
Is why we sing Oh Happy Day

Knowing his will
Is always used for good
We can't doubt his promises
Even if we could

The road less traveled
A highway it is
Full of his blessings
And the promises He fulfills

MR. LAW

You have made many laws
That deny freedom of speech
You have made many laws
That deny the right to teach

You have made many laws
To protect you from your fellow man
You have made many laws
For just a few
To use any way they can

You have made many laws
To keep the poor, poor
You have made many laws
Making life difficult for some to endure

You have made many laws to deny us
The freedom in which we can live
You have made many laws
Which respect is hard to give

It's not Mr. Law but God's Perfect Law
That should guide us every day
Being Hearers and Doers of his word
As we strive for His perfect way

LOVE CONQUERS ALL

Love is almighty
The end is never in sight
Love has the power
To fulfill your heart's delights.

Love is the perfect message
To send from your heart
Love is the meaning for us
To always make a new start

Love is the promise
We receive everyday
Love is the reason
We watch, look, and pray

It can move yonder mountain
It can calm a raging sea
So surely, wrapped in its arms
Is where we ought to be

Love Conquers all
The big and the small
In the promises to Abraham
Our blessings shall befall

PEACE

His presence in the storm
Is like a refreshing and calming balm
He knows what tomorrow holds
Wrapped in His loving arms

In the darkness of the night
He will make everything alright
With His broad wings of love
He overcomes Satan's might

Like the birds will always sing
Like the symbol of the wedding ring
There is no power on this earth
That can bring about our end

The Peace that exceeds understanding
When our fist are bound so tight
He then whispers in our ears
Perfect love is our hearts' delight

His Peace is wrapped in patience
And sprinkled with kindness and joy
If we walk in His authority
We'll enjoy life, reach for more

He will give us Peace
But only if we believe
All things are possible
With the faith of a mustard seed

A THINKER

What can power do
When a Thinker is born
Can power inject fear
Disbelief, confusion or scorn

What can power do
When a Thinker is born
Can it measure a Thinker's thoughts
Or can the Thinker's knowledge be bought

A Thinker reaches for higher ground
Knowing God makes the world go round
Power can do nothing but moan and frown
When Power sees God's Plan going down

You can count on one thing for sure
A Thinker will always endure
Knowing the race has been won
When He sacrificed his only Son

PUSH ON

People trying to make holes
That will close the doors
Of the will of God and hope

For good things to come
A brighter day
The little obstacles we can cope

When you push back
Don't give no slack
The door will open up more

You have been granted to know
That what is in store
Is what God has planned for you

When darkness comes
Just before the light
Take your pen and write
Keeping God always in sight

Look at the blessings
In all He has granted you
See His grace in all things
In life you have set out to do

And with His love
And all His grace
Thoughts of God
Will keep you in the race

UP JUMPS THE DEVIL

When you're travelling
The road of right
Up jumps the devil
With all of his might

He will torment the mind
Cause some sleepless nights
Using any tool
To keep God out of sight

He will jump up
In many fashions and forms
Using the hooks and charms
Of temptation's mighty arms

He uses frustration
To take our smile away
He will send the darkness
To mess up your day

He makes the people
Always want to fight
And do the many things
We know are just not right

Up jumps the devil
When travelling the road of right
God provides full armour
To turn his darkness into light

ALL WE NEED

All we need is to
Learn how to pray
Then our God will hear
Every word we say

All we need is to
Learn how to learn
This understanding can
Never bring us harm

All we need is to
Learn what to know
In God's presence
Worries pack up and go

All we need is to
Learn how to live
Then we'll understand
Why we have to give

All we need is to
Learn how to share
For in God's mind
Good is present everywhere

THE ART OF GIVING

When you find God
His spirit lives in your heart
The art of giving
Is one of your great rewards

To open our hearts
In spite of all wrongs
Gives a good feeling
And makes our hearts very strong

To share our mind
So that others may learn
Is the spirit of giving
A life worth living

To find in your mind
A heart made of gold
Gives you a feeling
Of being blessed and bold

When we conquer the greed
Of the foes at hand
We shall then live
In a very peaceful land

God gave us the power
Of peace of mind
Let no one strip you
Of this glory divine

Give your spirit
So that others may see
Master the art of giving
To reach your destiny

LOVE

Love is not just a four letter word
That comes from our mouths just to be heard
Love is a great blessing in life
Working together to overcome strife

Love is not blind
And just in our mind
Love is always perfect
Patient, true and kind

Love is the manner
In how we show we care
Love is the feeling
In our hearts we share

When you find love
Give love your best
This is God's way of showing
We are truly blessed

God gave us this blessing
To show to all
United we shall stand
But divided we will surely fall

CHECKED OUT OF CONFUSION

I checked out of confusion
Not a place for me
It dulls my senses
Can't reach my destiny

It's a sport practiced by many
It confounds my soul
But by God's Grace
He shows us our role

He gives a message
So loud and clear
His work and His wonders
Are beauty to my ear

I checked out of confusion
Ain't no light over there
Now I see clearly
God's blessings are everywhere

CLEAN UP

Clean up your own house
Leave others' house alone
You can't give me an answer
If your thinking is wrong

Clean up your own mind
You will have lasting grace
A clean mind is essential
For survival as a race

Clean up your own life
Let others not interfere
God has a plan for you
He is always standing near

Clean up your own house
And let it be seen
Then you can show others
What a clean house really means

ANGER

Anger controls the mind
Like a thief in the night
It will cause us to do and say things
We know are just not right

It is a great spirit
Becoming to the world
It will make your mind
Seem tossed and twirled

It is the number one enemy
To control the masses
It signs up students
To its many classes

It will destroy the good
And weak in heart
But if you guard with diligence
It will always part

God gave us a weapon
To keep it at bay
When He gave us the message
To watch, listen and pray

EVERYTHING HAS BALANCE

Everything has balance
To be perfect in his sight
Everything has balance
When to know what is right

He controls the wind and the waves
To our lost souls He saves
His Balance is in his Peace
So Blessings are always within reach

Everything has balance
To have wisdom is to have understanding
To Trust that his Love
Is not at all demanding

Everything has balance
To be perfect in his sight
We always want God's balance
At the center of our Life

A BETTER WAY

If you can't say something good
Say nothing at all
We can make the world better
With just a little smile

If you can't make someone happy
Don't try to make them sad
If you see that someone is good
Don't try to make them look bad

If you can't say thanks for
All He has done for you
Then reach into your mind
And find something good to do

If you can't say hello
Don't turn the other way
Share some love and kindness
In the words you choose to say

LET THEM TALK

Let them talk
For they know not what they say
Let them talk
Then show us the opposite way

Let them talk
Cause they surely can not hear
The promises of his glory
Let no man fear

As a thief in the night
With a bright shining light
God brings us his wisdom
Which is power and might

Let them talk
For they know not what they say
Let them talk
Til the great judgement day

When peace will surpass all understanding
And his love will be in our heart
And the blessings through Abraham
We will never ever part

EVIL

Evil surrounds us every day
All in the form of
Just getting in the way

Sharpen your skills
Always have great thoughts
This will strengthen you
And eliminate all doubts

Evil wears a smiling face
But evil has no lasting grace
It slips and slides in every crack
It pushes harder when you fight back

I say to evil
You can't keep the pace
God's grace and glory
Will always win the race

TEMPTATION

Temptation's out to get you
Everywhere you look
It stretches out it's arm
To use a mighty big hook

Temptation's out to get you
In everything you do
It creeps into an unguarded mind
Never having the time to renew

Temptation's strength is a mighty force
Trying to run you off your course
If we believe all that glitters is gold
We fell for the saddest story ever told

Keep God's favor in sight
Let blessings occupy your time
Then temptation won't try
To find it's way into your mind

MIGHTY DOLLAR

For those of you
Who think this way
That money will cure all ills
Have never seen the game that's played
With those mighty dollar bills

Money turns to evil
Once man has had his fill
He tries to control other people
With his mighty dollar bills

It has led many people
To the land where there is no hope
It has led many people
To use anything to help them cope

The dollar bill has given man
The instinct to want to kill
It has driven many men
From the top down a lonely hill

There is a God
And He is for real
He's got a cure
For the dollar bill's ills

JUST FOR ME

We must choose our words and be sincere
So our voice is heard loud and clear
And all with a listening ear
Will treasure our words and hold them dear

These are the best of times
But not for strong wine
For his word is the strength
To keep trouble from our Mind

We are more than just Conquerors
Traveling the road of life
We come to claim the victory
Not pain, Not sorrow, Not strife

And when we choose our words
Never walking in fear
Our Creator's Heavenly Voice
Resounds in our Ear

Love has been the Key
Throughout Eternity
With His blessing showering
Just for Me

THE TEACHER

What we need is not a Leader
What we need requires a Teacher

A Leader can lead us to battle fate
A Teacher can teach us to conquer hate

A Leader can lead us far astray
A Teacher will teach us
Truth in our heavenly father's way

A Leader will bear arms and fight
A Teacher wins with God's power and might

A Teacher the Leader is not, you see
But a Leader a Teacher can surely be

THOUGHTS

A flower can we grow
Without the rain water's flow
A mind can we reach
Without the tools to teach

A day can we see
Without wanting a sun that shines
Life's highway can we travel
Without a little time

A river cannot flow
Without a place to go
A picture cannot exist
Without a scene to show

A life can we live
Without wanting to give
Blessings do we deserve
If God we do not serve

GREATEST GIFT

What greater gift
Than a mind to think
What greater gift than
From the fountain of life to drink

What greater gift
Than outreaching hands
People helping others
To reach the promised land

What greater gift
Than an open mind and heart
Sharing with others
Where this love can start

What greater gift
Than the eyes to see
The rewards of this life
Reaching your destiny

What greater gift
Than our father above all
Granting us blessings
To always stand tall

FACE OF GOD

When we reach the mountain top
God shines his light on us
To be his chosen vessel
For all things in Him we trust

When we reach the mountain top
Wisdom and knowledge are clear
When He holds us in his arms
His loving voice is easy to hear

When we reach the mountain top
It's not the world we see
When we reach the mountain top
We see our Destiny

The Light God shines is brighter
It makes our burdens much lighter
Never believing in yourself
Our Heavenly Father always know best

HAPPINESS

Give a moment each day
To meditate in your heart
The joy God gives us
Each day before we start

Show a smile each day
With an alarming glow
Be thankful for the things
You have been granted to know

Have a kind and gentle heart
Pass judgment very light
Be very sure of what you do
Keep God's plan in your sight

Have faith in your beliefs
For faith is our relief
It will overcome
Your sorrows and your griefs

Let your conscience be your guide
No matter what people say
Let the reward of happiness
Always come into your day

YEAR OF JUBILEE

The Year of Jubilee
How pleasant to my ear
When I see God's presence
Reigning Far and Near

No Weapons No Powers
Can get in my path
My Vision is so clear
His promises forever last

All things are forgiven
Our minds are set free
He then sets our sights
As far as we can see

The Year of Jubilee
How pleasant to my ear
When I feel his presence
Reigning Far and Near

A WRITER'S SONG

An artist creates
A beautiful sight
A preacher gives a message
About the things that are right

A teacher creates thoughts
In the minds of others
A mother shows her children
How to Love one another

A tree gives breath
For man to live
Mankind's first thought should be
What Love can I give

A flower grows
From Mother Nature's Earth
God gave his only son
To grant us a chance for rebirth

God gives us Love
To know right from wrong
He grants us Peace
In the words of this Song

A KING

What makes a King
Is it the songs he sings
Is it his understanding of goodwill
And love to all men

Is it his Wisdom
That surpasses understanding
Or is it his courage to play
The last man standing

Is it his voice
That rings far and near
Or is it his voice
That makes all things clear

Is it his understanding
To always know the difference
Is it his authority
To always state his preference

Is it his Love for the Creator
Or Is it his understanding
Of how God grants him favor

Great is a King
Who is blessed with power and might
To rule his territory
With God's plan in sight

A QUEEN

A Queen rules her kingdom
With Love and everlasting might
From her tongue flows beauty
Because her God is always in sight

A Queen is honor and dignity
And her glow forever shines
She knows how to Love
And forever is very kind

A Queen never leaves
When the darkness turns to night
A Queen knows her beauty
Will turn darkness into light

A Queen knows her fate
Are the treasures and gifts of life
She knows her life's story
Is to be her Creator's glory

A Queen has treasures
Many may not see
She believes in God almighty
Always reaching her destiny

ABOUT THE AUTHOR

John Stuckey, Jr. has over forty years of experience as a Developer, Builder and Property Manager. His experience includes top-level professional experience as a Management Consultant and Strategic Planner. Mr. Stuckey has an extensive background in financial analysis, feasibility analysis, operations planning, staff management and strategic development planning with an emphasis in real estate development, acquisition and syndication.

Mr. Stuckey expanded his business operations to include the Mississippi/Louisiana Delta region of the country. He is responsible for the construction of 125 single-family homes and was awarded the honor of best Single-Family Tax Credit Housing Development in the State of Mississippi in 2007.

Mr. Stuckey and his wife Kemmeka manage numerous business ventures throughout several States. He is father to five children: Christy, Justin, Jason, Jerry and Carmen. He has one grandson, Tyree.

Visit us at jkdsoutreach.com 1-800-351-1195

www.ingramcontent.com/pod-product-compliance
Lightning Source LLC
Chambersburg PA
CBHW042042280426
43661CB00093B/961